From Home to School with Autism

by the same author

Making the Move
A Guide for Schools and Parents on the Transfer of Pupils with Autism Spectrum Disorders (ASDs) from Primary to Secondary School
K.I. Al-Ghani and Lynda Kenward
Illustrated by Haitham Al-Ghani
ISBN 978 1 84310 934 1

Learning About Friendship
Stories to Support Social Skills Training in Children with Asperger Syndrome and High Functioning Autism
K.I. Al-Ghani
Illustrated by Haitham Al-Ghani
ISBN 978 1 84905 145 3

The Red Beast
Controlling Anger in Children with Asperger's Syndrome
K.I. Al-Ghani
Illustrated by Haitham Al-Ghani
ISBN 978 1 84310 943 3

of related interest

Successful School Change and Transition for the Child with Asperger Syndrome
A Guide for Parents
Clare Lawrence
ISBN 978 1 84905 052 4

Working with Asperger Syndrome in the Classroom
An Insider's Guide
Gill D. Ansell
ISBN 978 1 84905 156 9

Count Me In!
Ideas for Actively Engaging Students in Inclusive Classrooms
Richard Rose and Michael Shevlin
Foreword by Paul Cooper
Innovative Learning for All Series
ISBN 978 1 84310 955 6

Reaching and Teaching the Child with Autism Spectrum Disorder
Using Learning Preferences and Strengths
Heather MacKenzie
ISBN 978 1 84310 623 4

Common SENse for the Inclusive Classroom
How Teachers Can Maximise Existing Skills to Support Special Educational Needs
Richard Hanks
ISBN 978 1 84905 057 9

From Home to School with Autism

How to Make Inclusion a Success

K.I. Al-Ghani and Lynda Kenward
Illustrated by Haitham Al-Ghani

Jessica Kingsley *Publishers*
London and Philadelphia

First published in 2011
by Jessica Kingsley Publishers
116 Pentonville Road
London N1 9JB, UK
and
400 Market Street, Suite 400
Philadelphia, PA 19106, USA

www.jkp.com

Library of Congress Cataloging in Publication Data
Al-Ghani, K. I.
From home to school with autism : how to make inclusion a success / K.I. Al-Ghani and Lynda Kenward ; illustrated by Haitham Al-Ghani.
p. cm.
ISBN 978-1-84905-169-9 (alk. paper)
1. Autistic children--Education. I. Kenward, Lynda. II. Al-Ghani, Haitham. III. Title.
LC4717.A39 2010
371.94--dc22
2010026390

British Library Cataloguing in Publication Data
A CIP catalogue record for this book is available from the British Library

ISBN 978 1 84905 169 9

Printed and bound in Great Britain by
MPG Books Group

From Lynda

This book is dedicated to my mother, Barbara, and my son, Alexander, for their love, care and support.

From Kay and Haitham

This book is dedicated to Ahmed and Sarah Al-Ghani for their continued love, support and encouragement.

Contents

Preface

Starting school is a major step in the life of any child.

For children with an Autism Spectrum Disorder (ASD) the start of school life can be marred by days full of confusion and high anxiety as they strive to make sense of their new surroundings.

By implementing strategies before the big day and preparing the child well in advance, the transition from home to school can be achieved with minimal stress and disruption for everyone concerned.

It is preparation, planning and a positive partnership between home and school that can make this phase in the child's life meaningful and fun.

For those schools striving to give a suitable provision for every child, the suggestions outlined in this book can help to ensure an autism-friendly classroom, which will result in successful inclusion. It is our belief that all children will benefit from a visual and structured approach to the school day. It is our hope that all those who work with children with an ASD will value the book's practical solutions and find them simple to implement.

1 Introduction

Quite often the first alarm bells regarding the child's diagnosis of ASD are heard at pre-school or a crèche. It is here that teachers and teaching assistants (TAs) may have noticed that something is 'not quite right' with the child. It may be:

- a delay in language
- an inability to follow instructions
- too many temper tantrums
- a need for the child to be alone and following his or her own agenda
- a lack of eye contact
- poor shared attention
- repetitive/stereotyped play activities
- difficulty in accepting change
- obsessive behaviours.

Whatever it is that has alerted the staff, it will often lead to a visit to either the GP, health visitor, social worker, speech and language therapist, pathologist, educational psychologist or other health care worker – or a combination of these professionals.

Following a diagnosis, a child will quite possibly attend a mainstream school if he or she has:

- Asperger Syndrome (AS) – Child has an IQ above 85 with *no* language delay
- High Functioning Autism (HFA) – Child has an IQ above 85 but *with* language delay
- PDD-NOS (Pervasive Developmental Disorder – Not Otherwise Specified) – some autistic traits seen.

There has been a shift in the policies concerning inclusion over the last ten years. Schools are aware of the need to make allowances for children with special needs, but understanding of ASDs can still be sadly lacking. In our work as Specialist Advisory Teachers for Inclusion Support we have often been called into schools to help when things start to 'go wrong'. It is our hope that this book will help to pave the way for children with an ASD starting school, so that things 'go right' from the outset.

Sometimes there are children starting school with an undiagnosed ASD and so those first few days, until routines are established, can be a testing time for everyone. It is our premise that the strategies outlined in this book could be implemented in every pre-school/reception classroom. They would be of benefit to all children – not just those with an ASD.

2 First Steps

It should be acknowledged that the real experts on a child with an ASD are always the parents/caregivers, and so a strong partnership between home and school forms the basis of any successful programme for transition.

The school should analyse its inclusion policy and ensure that it provides information based on the following frequently asked parent questions:

- Are there any children with ASDs in school?

- Are staff trained to work with children with ASDs?

- Are you able to give staff time off to attend training courses in ASD?

- What is the ratio of staff to children?

- What facilities do you have that would be appropriate for children with ASDs? For example, in-house swimming pool, sensory room, quiet withdrawal areas, security measures (e.g. locked gates, high handles on doors, etc.).

- What are the school arrangements for: start of the day; playtimes; lunch times; home times?

- How flexible is the timetable/daily organisation?

- Would staff be able to do a home visit to see the child in this setting?

- Does the school have staggered starts at the beginning of the school year?

- Would the staff be able to implement a home/school liaison diary?

3 The Importance of Good Communication

Communication is the key to a successful transition. Good communication will help to foster a better understanding and influence the response to any given situation.

Parents can best support the school by showing that they care about all the children, not just their own. It could be part of the school's inclusion policy to invite parents of children with ASDs to help with fund raising; join the PTA; meet the school Board of Governors; have opportunities to volunteer for field trips or special occasions. By extending this hand to the parents it will make them feel less anxious about their child and it will help them to demonstrate a concern for all the people involved with educating their child. In this way, all those involved can maintain a positive attitude, expect the best from each other and ensure that school life is pleasurable for every child as well as for the child struggling with an ASD.

4 How the Parents/ Caregivers Can Help the School

There are many ways in which the caregiver can help the school to accommodate the child. The school could suggest these to prospective parents:

Prepare a Pupil Profile

This should be filled out by the parent/caregiver and given to the school as soon as the placement has been finalised.

The Pupil Profile

This is ....

attach photo here

....'s birthday is on..

He/she is ....years old.

In ....'s family there are ....

....

....

....

attach family photo here

.... has a pet ....

....

....

attach photo/s here

..........................'s favourite foods are ....

....

....

..........................'s favourite toys are ....

....

....

..........................'s favourite TV programmes/DVDs are ....

....

....

.....................................has some medical problems:
(list condition plus any medications)

....

....

.....................................has some sensory problems:

.....................................is distressed

by the sound of ....

....

....

by the smell of ....

....

....

by the taste of ....

....

....

by the sight of ....

....

....

by the feel of ....

....

....

When...........................is distressed he/she ....

....

....

....

.............................is calmed by ....

....

....

✓

..................................finds it difficult to *(tick as appropriate)*

☐ get dressed

☐ fasten shoes

☐ go to the toilet

☐ eat snack/lunch

☐ ask for something

☐ take turns

☐ share toys

☐ follow instructions

Other ....

Add any other information you think the school would find useful:

....

....

....

....

....

.... is good at

....

....

....

....

....

....

Contact telephone numbers:

Home: ....

Work: ....

Mobile phone: ....

E-mail address: ....

Postal address: ....

....

Sample Pupil Profile

This is ....Haitham Al-Ghani...........

.............Haitham............'s birthday is on.........19th July...............

He/~~she~~ is ....five.........years old.

In ....Haitham.......'s family there are ....3 people...............

His father who he calls 'Baba'

His mother who he calls 'Mama'

His sister who he calls 'Dada' or 'Sarah'

Haitham .... has a pet .... hamster called Dodger ....

2 goldfish called Rock and Roll ....

2 turtles called Sally and Sidney ....

attach photo/s here

.... Haitham .... 's favourite foods are ....

chicken nuggets, white bread, grapes, tomato ketchup, ...

smarties and milk. ....

.... Haitham .... 's favourite toys are .... dinosaurs, ...

his stuffed frog, toy cars, monkeys ....

....

.... Haitham .... 's favourite TV programmes/DVDs are ....

Thomas the Tank Engine, Postman Pat, Jungle Book ....

....

...............Haitham................. has some medical problems:
(list condition plus any medications)

Eczema
....

....

..............Haitham................. has some sensory problems:

..............Haitham................. is distressed

by the sound of ....the vacuum cleaner, aeroplanes, most

unexpected loud noises
....

....

by the smell of............petrol fumes, coffee

....

....

by the taste of.....................N/A

....

....

by the sight of .... dogs ....

....

....

by the feel of............... labels in clothes, buttons on shirts ....

....

....

When...... Haitham ......is distressed he/~~she~~ ...... screams, ...

covers his ears, goes under the table, runs up and down, cries

quietly..

....

...... Haitham ...... is calmed by ...... watching favourite ....

films; removing from stimuli; distracting with favourite toy;

cuddling in a rocking chair with someone singing 'Simple

Simon'...

.......Haitham.............finds it difficult to *(tick as appropriate)*

☐ get dressed

☐ fasten shoes

☐ go to the toilet

☐ eat snack/lunch

☑ ask for something

☑ take turns

☑ share toys

☑ follow instructions

Other .....moving from one activity to another.....

Add any other information you think the school would find useful:

Haitham has no real sense of danger and may run away if he

sees something he wants. He is fascinated by children crying

and will sometimes look at them closely and laugh.

....

....

.............Haitham............is good at

doing puzzles...

riding a bicycle (with stabilisers)....................

singing nursery rhymes...................................

saying the alphabet...

drawing..

....

Contact telephone numbers:

Home: ....

Work: ....

Mobile phone: ....

E-mail address: ....

Postal address: ....

....

Home visual schedule

Introduce a visual schedule at home. This will assist continuity and consistency of approach. The school could make up a home symbol pack to give to prospective parents of children with ASDs.

See home symbols on pp.30–31 to photocopy and put together a full day schedule.

The 'Happy Scrap Book'

Encourage parents/caregivers to create a 'Happy Scrap Book'. This is something the child can look at in moments of anxiety. It could contain photos or samples of any or all of the following:

Favourite:

- pastimes/interests/hobbies
- books
- DVDs/TV programmes
- music
- colours
- smells/textures
- pets
- people
- food
- places
- toys.

Home Symbols

sit	look	listen
toilet	bath	sleep
walking	visitor	car
bus	sticker	choose

Home Symbols

5 The Home/ School Liaison

The Starting School Book

The aim of this book is to prepare the child with an ASD for the monumental changes associated with starting school. It helps by introducing the new environment in a visual, clear and comprehensible way.

Constructing the book

- Each phrase should be on a different page and written at the bottom, with a space for a photograph or symbol above.

- The following list provides examples of possible book entries. It is not necessary to use all sections. Key information rather than quantity is more relevant for a child with an ASD.

- 'My' can be replaced by the child's name, if preferred. (Children with HFA may still be experiencing difficulties with use of personal pronouns.)

- When introducing/compiling the book, talk to the child about each page. For example, when discussing the 'My Classroom' page, talk about the other children, the resources, classroom areas, wall displays, etc.

- Aim to finish with a positive. Ensure that the last page includes an aspect of school life that the child will enjoy (see sample).

- The book could be photocopied on coloured paper, such as cream, in the case of visual sensitivity.

My Starting School Book

attach photo of child here

1

attach photo/s here

My school

2

attach photo/s here

My teacher/s

3

✓

attach photo/s here

My helper/s (assistant/s)

4

attach photo/s here

My classroom

5

✓

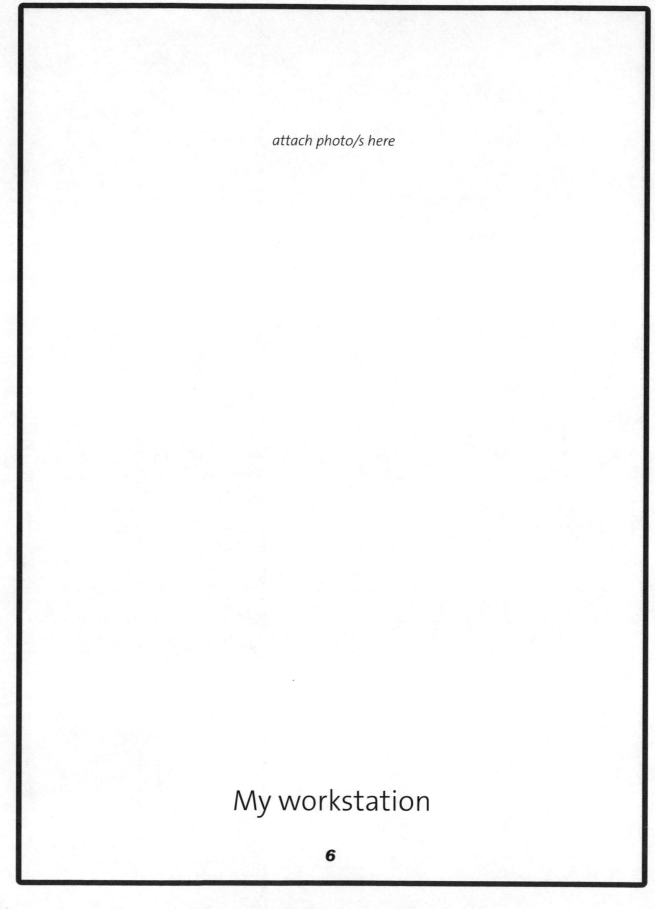

attach photo/s here

My workstation

6

attach photo/s here

My timetable

7

✓

attach photo/s here

My peg

8

attach photo/s here

The playground

9

41

attach photo/s here

The toilet area

10

attach photo/s here

The hall

11

✓

attach photo/s here

Classroom toys

12

The Starting School Book should be completed in stages during and between each school visit.

Additional pages may need to be included or some excluded, as appropriate, to meet a child's individual needs, circumstances and previous experiences.

During each visit, take photographs of key areas, staff, etc. for the book. If possible, allow the child to take these.

Reinforcing consistencies

From home to school

Consider:

- visual labels
- visual timetable
- other visual resources
- general resources such as games, toys, etc.
- activities
- friends
- 'adult only' areas.

From pre-school to school

As above, plus:

- workstation
- individual needs assistant (INA)/TA/support staff
- school entrance/exit
- routines:
  - playtimes
  - playgrounds
  - lunch time
  - breaks

o starting time

o beginning and end of the day

o P.E.

o assemblies

o timetable

o school/class rules

o reward system.

Possible changes

Consider:

- routines (as above)
- staffing – teaching and support staff
- pupils/groups
- uniform
- environment:

  o classroom

  o position of workstation within the new classroom

  o areas – subject/storage

  o resources and their location

  o furniture

  o school/class entrance/exit

  o cloakroom/peg/toilets.

Suggested photographs

- playground
- dining hall/assembly hall
- classroom door with class name/number

- teacher
- support staff
- class rules
- school entrance/exit
- inside: classroom/areas/resources/key labels
- peg/cloakroom.

The book should be completed as soon as possible after a firm school placement has been made. It should be available for the child to re-visit at any time during the summer break, even while away on holiday.

6 Starting School Procedures

As soon as the school placement is confirmed, the child should visit the school on several occasions, with a parent or caregiver, to view the environment and meet key staff. This should be broken down into stages, for example:

- Introduce the Starting School Book. Make this a relaxed experience and perhaps start with just the picture of the school. Combine with the 'School' pictorial narrative (see p.76).

- Visit the school gate to view the building.

- Visit the entrance hall to look at the display boards.

- Visit the classroom and cloakroom area, if adjacent. This may need to be immediately before or after school, when the classroom is empty. A further visit should be arranged to observe the working classroom.

- Meet the teacher, TA or INA working within the classroom and, if possible, other key members of staff.

- Visit the wider school environment, such as the dining hall, playground, etc.

For some children, additional visits, or alternative arrangements, may be necessary to break down the above into smaller steps.

We advise that each page of the Starting School Book should be laminated, joined by treasury tags and the photographs attached by Velcro® or Blu-tack®. It is an invaluable and re-usable resource as a 'New Class Book' for introducing the consistencies and changes of the annual class move. Pages can be added or removed, as appropriate, and photographs replaced by symbols, as the child progresses. Also, the book can be introduced to the whole class, to prepare all children for the transition.

As advisory teachers for children with ASDs in mainstream schools, we have witnessed the success of this strategy. Anxieties and apprehensions have been reduced and often eliminated, allowing a smooth and stress-free transition for the child, parents/caregivers and school staff.

7 Visual Support in the Classroom

Most children with an ASD find it difficult to process verbal information and therefore it is essential to use visual methods to aid children's understanding.

Some examples of effective visual supports follow. Photocopiable symbols for use in these supports can be found on pp.59–62.

- A visual timetable showing the main events throughout the school day.

- An individual timetable to show specific tasks or the order of a task.

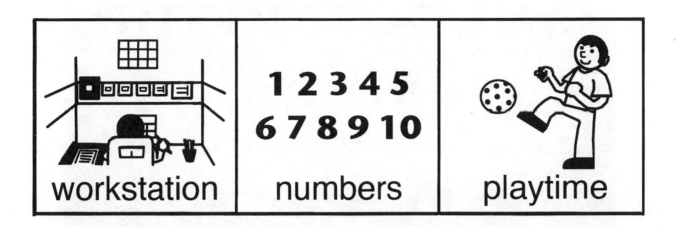

- A 'first this and then that' strip for a child who is difficult to motivate. (To simplify you could say 'NOW'/'THEN'.)

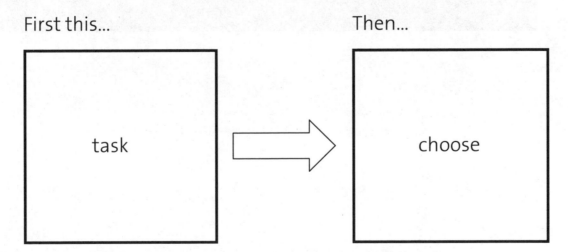

● Transition visuals (p.66) and sand timers.
● An individual workstation.

- Classroom labels on cupboards, equipment, areas, etc.

- A days of the week board (see p.58).
  (Train the child to do this every day and have one at home also — concepts of time are very difficult for children with ASDs.)

- Pictorial narratives (see Chapter 13).
  Where appropriate, signs and symbols may be used to supplement speech.

- Motivation boards (see pp.55–57).

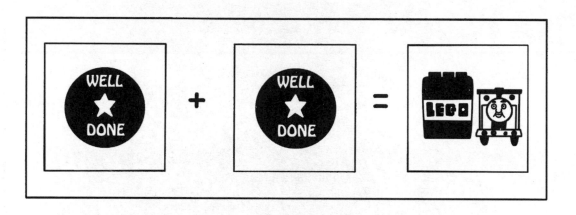

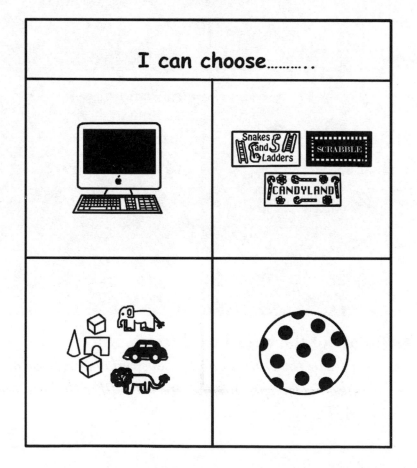

Motivation Boards

I can choose...	
Affix photo or symbol	Affix photo or symbol
Affix photo or symbol	Affix photo or symbol

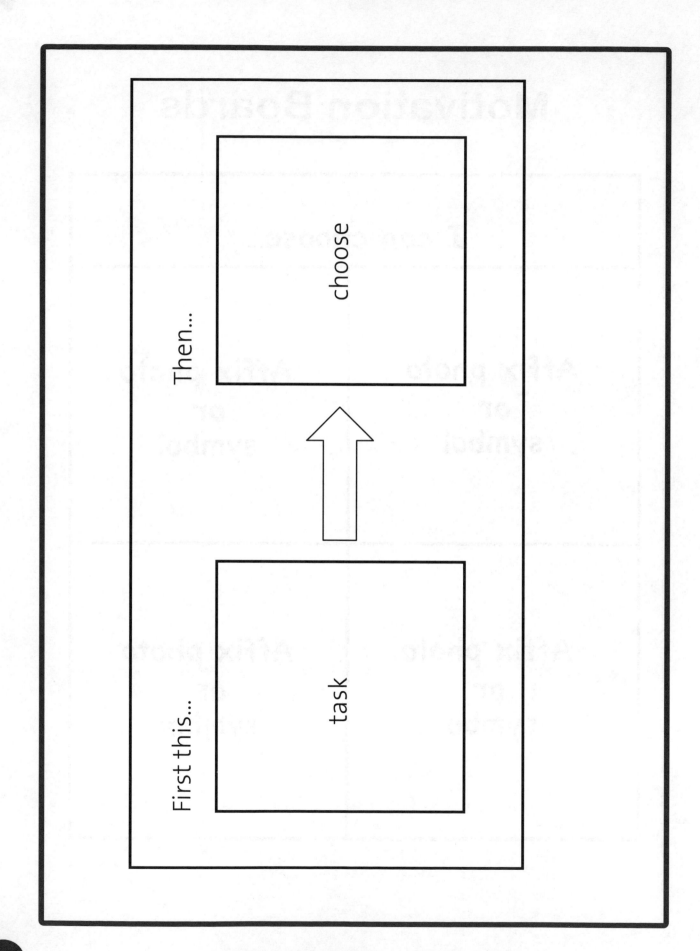

First this...

task

Then...

choose

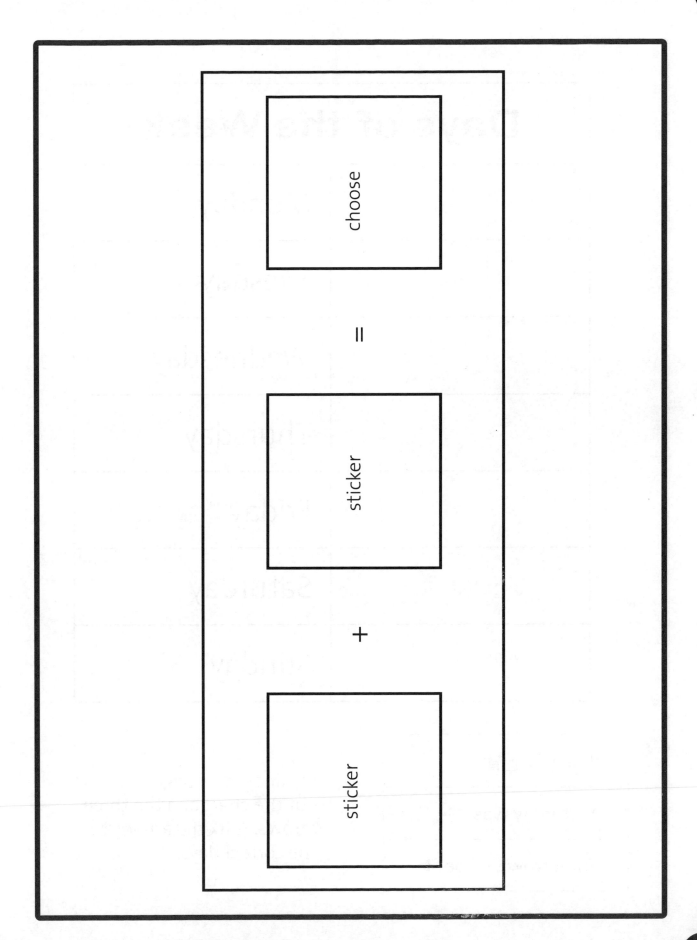

sticker + sticker = choose

Days of the Week

	Monday
	Tuesday
	Wednesday
	Thursday
	Friday
	Saturday
	Sunday

Today is ☞

Yesterday was →

Tomorrow will be ▶

Laminate this page then cut out the chart and the three arrows. Affix the arrows to the correct days.

School Symbols

workstation	work	playtime
group work	painting	choose
good looking	good listening	good sitting
good learning	good singing	numbers

School Symbols

 literacy	1 2 3 4 5 + − × ÷ = numeracy	 register
 history	 cut and stick	 writing
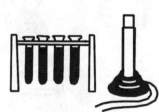 science	 RE	 computer
 reading	 geography	 packed lunch

School Symbols

task 1	task 2	task 3
home	games	trip/outing
toys	reward box	music
snack time	drink	time out

School Symbols

assembly	making	cooking
swimming	gym	dancing
role-play	turn taking	nurse
dentist	doctor	talking

Adapting the symbols

For Foundation Stage Curriculum in the Early Years (UK), School Symbols and Home Symbols (see pp.30–31) can be adapted to fit the six areas of learning and development.

Communication/language and literacy

Use symbols for literacy, writing, reading, listening and talking but cover over the text before photocopying and laminating. When the child reaches Key Stage 1, the text may be introduced to ensure continuity and develop new vocabulary.

Problem solving, reasoning and numeracy

Use symbols for number, numeracy and computer (I.T.).

Knowledge and understanding of the world

Geography, history, science, R.E., making (later adapt this to read 'D.T.').

Personal and social development

Trip/outing, assembly, turn taking, choose, workstation, group work, good sitting/listening/looking/learning, wash, brush teeth, brush hair (for personal hygiene), packed lunch/dinner (for table etiquette/social skills).

Physical development

Walk, gym, swimming, playtime.

Creative development

Painting, making, role play, singing, cooking.

Kindergarten and elementary curriculum in the USA

Similarly, the symbols can be adapted to fit in with the six areas of learning used in schools in the USA. Symbols can be photocopied without text, with text, in another language if necessary and using local terminology, for example, 'recess' for 'playtime'.

Personal and social development

Trip/outing, assembly, turn taking, choose, workstation, group work, good sitting/listening/looking/learning, dress, packed lunch, dinner, doctor, nurse, dentist.

Language

Listen, talking, good listening, literacy (these symbols can be adapted to read 'stories' or 'books'), reading, writing.

Mathematics

Number (this can be adapted to read 'counting'), numeracy and computer (I.T.).

Science and technology

Science, computer, making.

Health and physical activities

Wash, brush teeth, brush hair, doctor, nurse, dentist, walk, gym, swimming, playtime (recess).

The arts

Painting, making, role play, good singing, cooking, music.

Supporting Transitions at Home and School

Any way you look at it, transition plus autism equals anxiety. How do you get a child, deeply engrossed in his or her favourite pastime and enjoying a rare moment of relaxation, to move to a different activity?

This is where you use the 'transition trains'. You become the Signal Master or Fat Controller – put on your cap, give a short burst on a whistle (if the child is not sound sensitive!) and hold up the card. First, you or the child will need to colour the trains photocopied from the template on the next page.

Green train signals GO AHEAD (enjoy yourself).

Orange train signals the activity is about to finish, so SLOW DOWN – use this with a 5 or 2 minute sand timer.

Red train means it is time to STOP – ALL CHANGE.

Once the children become used to this system they really enjoy it and it becomes part of the fun.

Ensure that the child knows he or she will be doing next (visual timetable) immediately after showing the red train.

Then it is all aboard to the next activity – whether it be bed or bath time at home or time to do some busy work at school.

Transition Trains

Colour, cut out and laminate.

9 The 'Good Job Log Book'

It is never too early in school life to start to build self-esteem. The more able children with AS or HFA will benefit greatly from having their accomplishments listed as a means to:

- foster feelings of pride and happiness

- gain understanding of positive emotions

- produce a positive real life memory bank (RLMB)

- change their mood if they are starting to feel anxious.

This book is also a useful tool for reflection after the rigours of the school year. Sometimes we lose sight of what has been achieved when we are always navigating the next hurdle.

Sample page

Date:	Susie…	At school…	At home…	I felt…
25/12/09	did a poo in the toilet	Mrs Marsh gave me a sticker	Mum said…	

As child gets older

Date:	I...	At school...	At home...	I felt...
25/12/11	waited in line	the dinner lady told my teacher and I got time on the computer	Mum said I could have an extra 10 minutes of TV	proud excited happy relaxed

Positive emotions

Happy, Proud, Relieved, Excited, Amused, Relaxed, Confident, Encouraged, Hopeful.

Disclosure: Who Needs to Know?

It should always be the parents'/caregivers' prerogative when it comes to disclosure. They should be considered important members of the educational team and so need to be consulted about any issues that will affect their child.

A meeting should be held to list those individuals who will need to know that a child has an ASD.

As well as the head teacher, special educational needs coordinator (SENCO), class teacher, TAs and INAs you should consider:

- visiting professionals
- the music teacher
- dinner supervisors
- taxi/bus drivers
- the school nurse
- the school secretary
- the site manager
- voluntary workers
- the children.

Avoiding Trouble in the Classroom

Teachers can avoid behavioural difficulties in the classroom by ensuring they can answer 'yes' to the following questions:

- Has the classroom got a clear visual timetable with a moving arrow to show the passage of time?

- Has the child got a personal timetable to show a breakdown of tasks?

- Are you ensuring that the child understands any given task and that he or she has the skills to do the task?

- Is the child being rewarded frequently for finishing tasks and for behaving well?

- Has the classroom got clearly marked areas so the child will understand what activities are acceptable in each area?

- Are transition times signalled clearly in advance?

- Are you supplementing instructions with visual signs or symbols if appropriate?

- Has the child got visual reminders of key rules, for example, **Good Sitting**, **Good Listening**, **Good Looking = Good Learning**?

- Has the child got sufficient personal space?

- Has the child got a clearly marked place to sit, work and keep possessions?

- Are all staff consistent in their approach to any undesirable behaviour?

- Can the child go to a quiet area if he or she is feeling anxious?

- Have you got a selection of fidget toys and weighted knee mats for children who find it difficult to sit still for any length of time?

- Have you consulted the parents about possible strategies to use if the child becomes upset or non-compliant?

- Are the children in the class aware of the special needs children? (You will need parental permission for this.)

Top Tips for Teaching Assistants

It is quite likely that a child with an ASD in the mainstream classroom will have an INA or TA. This job is never an easy one and so the school should strive to make these members of staff feel valued and supported.

Here are our top tips for TAs:

To encourage good behaviours use the power of 'positive praise'; tell children what you like about their work, appearance or attitude. Just saying 'well done' is not as effective as using positive praise. (Remember that some children love over-the-top American style praise but others are embarrassed by it, so gear it to the child. Some children with ASDs hate to be praised, so instead of saying, 'That was brilliant!' say, 'I wish I had thought of that!')

Timers are a great tool to use in class – especially during transition times such as lining up, tidy table time, change of activity time, etc. For example: 'It is almost lunch time so we need to tidy our tables. I am setting the timer for five minutes – let's see who can tidy up before the sand goes down.' Now you have turned a 'pupil against teacher' activity into a 'pupil against timer' activity – effective and fun!

Children with ASDs need the 4 Rs:

ROUTINE – RITUAL – REPETITION – RESOURCES.

Establish routines for transition times, incorporate special interests into your reinforcers to encourage rituals, give plenty of opportunities to repeat actions and use visual resources whenever possible.

Finally, we who teach children with ASDs know that we are only as good as our reinforcers! These children are not as motivated by natural reinforcers like praise and the feeling of a job well done, so we need to use our ingenuity to think up some artificial motivators. Here are some that work well.

1. A snack (mini boxes of raisins, grapes, carrot sticks, fruit flakes, etc. – check for allergies and that they are okay with parents).

2. Stickers/happy faces/laminated tokens of favourite characters, such as Doctor Who, Scooby Doo, Thomas the Tank Engine, etc.

3. The good child 'bank account' – paper money used and added up at the end of the week to 'spend' in the teacher's 'shop'.

4. Extra preferred activity time.

5. A special book/game to take home over the weekend.

6. A homework pass (for the older child).

7. Reading a story with a special adult/choosing the story for story time.

8. The 'Good Job Box' – filled with interesting and exciting things the child may enjoy. The children can earn time in the box by doing work tasks independently, having a good playtime, doing good transitioning, etc. This can promote independence and positively encourage good behaviour. (See 'Good Job Box' pictorial narrative on p.81.)

9. A 'time with the head teacher/principal' token (to be negotiated with the head, of course). Most heads would love to have 'good' children sent to them instead of those in trouble. Indeed, the head could invite a small group for a special treat.

10. Teacher's special helper badge.

The key to managing challenging behaviour in children with ASDs, is to be prepared. Know exactly what you are going to do in advance, use minimal speech and show minimal emotion:

- **Less talk – less emotion** – then remember:

- **Praise the best – Ignore the rest**.

('Ignore the rest' means take control but do not mention the behaviour; as soon as you mention a behaviour you reinforce it. It is much better to take control, distract and re-direct.)

Pictorial Narratives

For young children with ASDs the use of a pictorial narrative can be an aid to understanding. When read over a number of days it can help the child to prepare for daily events in school life.

1. School
2. The teacher
3. The children
4. Different adults
5. Assembly
6. Playtime
7. Wet playtimes
8. My peg
9. The toilet area
10. Visitors
11. The workstation
12. Lunch time (dinner time)
13. Sharing classroom toys
14. The reward/treat/activity board
15. The 'Good Job Box'

These narratives should have one sentence/phrase per page, together with a photograph. (They can be word processed on cream-coloured paper, in the case of visual sensitivity.)

The phrases below are examples, and you should change the gender and number of people described according to the children or adults in your photographs.

1. School

This is my school.
My school has:

an entrance hall

classrooms (this is my classroom) *(attach photo)*

an assembly hall

a playground

toilets

a swimming pool

a library

lots of children

a head teacher/principal

adults to help me.

2. The teacher

Here is my teacher. *(attach photo)*

His name is…

Teachers help children to learn.

My teacher will help me.

He will use pictures/photographs/symbols to show me what to do.

3. The children

Children go to school.

There are lots of children at my school.

Children belong to classes.

There are many children in my class.

This is my friend. *(attach photo)*

His name is…

He will be in my class.

4. Different adults

Sometimes my teacher is not at school.

Sometimes I have a different teacher.

She will know about my workstation.

She will know what I like.

She will have pictures/photographs/symbols to help me.

She will know all about me.

5. Assembly

Sometimes (on Fridays…) we have a school assembly.

This is where we go for assembly. *(attach photo)*

There are lots of children at assembly time.

The children sit quietly.

The children listen to the speaker (teacher/principal/visitor).

Sometimes the children sing together.

When assembly is finished we go back to the classroom.

My helper will tell me when it is time to go back to the classroom.

6. Playtime

This is my school playground. *(attach photo)*

At playtimes we go into the playground.

Some children play games with friends.

Some children play on their own.

Some children like to sit on the bench.

These are adults who will help me at playtime. *(attach photo)*

The teacher/playground helper will show me the red 'stop train' when playtime is finished.

7. Wet playtimes

Sometimes it rains.

Sometimes it rains at playtime.

When it rains at playtime we stay in the classroom.

The children can choose books or toys.

My teacher will show me my choice board.

The teacher will show me the 'stop train' when playtime is over.

8. My peg

Here is the cloakroom *(attach photo)*

This is my (or [name of child]'s) peg *(attach photo)*

On my peg I can hang:

my coat

my hat

my scarf

my P.E. bag

my lunch box

my book bag.

9. The toilet area

Here is the toilet area. *(attach photo)*

The girls' toilet.

The boys' toilet.

The wash basins.

The soap.

The paper towels.

My toilet symbol/picture/photograph. *(attach photo)*

10. Visitors

Sometimes people come to the classroom/school.

They are called visitors.

They look at the classroom/school/playground.

They watch the children work and play.

They talk to the teacher.

Sometimes they will look at my workstation.

Sometimes they will look at my symbols/pictures/photographs.

11. The workstation

This is my (or [name of child]'s) workstation. *(attach photo)*

At my workstation I have:

my timetable

my choice board

my trays

my pencil pot

symbols/pictures/photographs.

Sometimes I work at my workstation with…

12. Lunch time (dinner time)

This is where I will eat my lunch. *(attach photo)*

We eat lunch in the dining hall.

We sit at tables.

Some children have a school lunch/dinner.

Some children have a packed lunch/dinner.

I will have a…

My helper (name) will show me what to do when I have eaten my lunch.

13. Sharing classroom toys

These are some classroom toys. *(attach photo)*

Sometimes I want to play with the same toy as another child.

Here is my wait/taking turns symbol/picture/photograph. *(attach photo)*

My teacher will use a sand timer to help me to wait for my turn.

My teacher will show me the green 'go train' when it is my turn to play with the toy.

My teacher will show me the red 'stop train' when it is someone else's turn to play with the toy.

14. The reward/treat/activity board

On my board are four (or other number) squares.

I can put a sticker in the square for good working/good sitting/ good listening.

The teacher/helper will tell me when I can put a sticker on my board.

When I get all the stickers I can choose a reward/treat/activity.

15. The 'Good Job Box'

Here is the 'Good Job Box'. *(attach photo)*

Inside the box are things I like.

I like colouring/reading/music/modelling/Lego™, etc.

When I fill my sticker board I can choose to play with the things in the box for…minutes.

The teacher will show me the red 'stop train' when it is time to put the things back in the box.

14 Troubleshooting

When working with children with ASDs, forewarned is forearmed! Our many years of experience have shown us that certain difficulties are almost inevitable. Being prepared is the key to success. For this reason we have devised a list of preparation strategies and possible difficulties that may be encountered in the following areas:

1. New class

2. Start of day

3. School assemblies

4. Playtimes

5. Play/activity/choosing times

6. P.E. lessons/gym class

7. Swimming lessons

8. Obsessions

9. Staffing changes

10. End of term/school year

1. New class

How to prepare the child

Break routines down into small steps. Stages can be omitted, combined, repeated or adapted to meet individual needs.

Add the relevant symbols to the strip to introduce each stage.

Rewards should be used to motivate and reinforce appropriate behaviour.

Stage 1 Read a pictorial narrative about moving into a new class. Introduce the symbol cards and prepare the child for a visit to the new classroom.

Stage 2 Visit the classroom, when it is empty, to look at areas. Discuss the location of the workstation.

Stage 3 Visit the classroom to meet the new teacher and any other staff. Take photographs (let the child do this if possible).

Stage 4 Make a book with the photographs. Talk about the different routines or rules. Share it with the child as often as needed.

Stage 5 Move the workstation to the new classroom and allow the child to help set it up or view it.

Stage 6 Allow the child to take the book home to share it with his or her family members.

What you might need

Symbol cards for:

> walk
>
> new classroom
>
> photographs
>
> book
>
> workstation
>
> teacher
>
> classroom or cloakroom areas – for example, peg, toilet.

Strip to attach symbols.

Camera to take photographs of new teacher, classroom, areas of the classroom, children, TA.

'New Class' book.

Pictorial narrative.

Problems you may experience

THE CHILD DOES NOT WANT TO ENTER THE NEW ROOM.

Walk the child to view the classroom door and look inside the room when there are no children in the room.

Ensure that there are familiar things or faces in the new classroom, for example, favourite resources, the TA.

Move the workstation or set up an identical one, before the visit.

THE NEW CLASS RULES AND ROUTINES ARE DIFFERENT.

Make visual resources to show the rules and routines. Introduce them and then take the child on a visit to the classroom to see them in action with the current class.

THE CHILD IS CONCERNED ABOUT MEETING DIFFERENT CHILDREN IN THE NEW CLASS.

Take photographs of some of the new children. Add these to the book. Allow these children to accompany the child to show him or her around the new classroom. Allow the child to join the new children at playtimes.

THE CHILD IS CONCERNED ABOUT DIFFERENT RESOURCES IN THE NEW ROOM.

Ensure that there are some familiar resources in the new room.

Borrow resources and allow the child to use them in more familiar surroundings and then return them to the new classroom.

THE CHILD WON'T SHARE THE PICTORIAL NARRATIVE.

Make the 'New Class' book and introduce it in place of the pictorial narrative. Allow other children to share it.

Invite family members to share it at home.

You may need to make two copies.

THE CHILD REMAINS ANXIOUS AFTER THE STAGES HAVE BEEN WORKED THROUGH.

Repeat the stages as necessary. If possible, allow the child to visit the new classroom during the school holiday or just before the change – maybe during a staff training day. Allow the child to take the pictorial narrative and/or the 'New Class' book with him or her on the first day.

THE CHILD DOESN'T WANT TO LEAVE THE NEW CLASSROOM.

Suggest that the child borrows resources from the new classroom.

Use a sand timer or transition trains to prepare for leaving.

THE CHILD IS CONCERNED ABOUT THE DIFFERENT TOILET AREA.

Use photographs and allow the child to use the toilet during each visit to the new classroom.

Ensure that a familiar symbol strip for the toileting routine is placed in the toilet area.

Reward use of the toilet.

THE CHILD LEAVES THE CLASS WITHOUT PERMISSION.

Place a wide sticky-back strip on the carpet in front of the classroom door.

Explain by using a pictorial narrative that children are not allowed to cross the line without an adult.

2. Start of day

How to prepare the child

Stage 1 Identify a highly motivating activity or task for arrival/settling in.

Stage 2 Introduce a pictorial sequence for the start of the school day procedure, for example, hang coat, lunch box on shelf, workstation. Read a pictorial narrative, if additional explanation is required. Reinforce the entry workstation activity and explain the length of time allowed for this. Attach the sequence to the child's peg or place it in the workstation. Support the child until he or she can follow this independently. Reward successes, as appropriate.

Stage 3 Set up the sand timer or transition trains. Allow the child the agreed time with the settling in activity.

Stage 4 Use the sand timer or transition trains to indicate the end of the activity. Go through the visual timetable for the morning/day or set it up together. Allow the child to join the class at an appropriate time.

Give the child a verbal warning, while referring to the visual indicator, prior to the end of activity time.

What you might need

Symbol cards or photographs for sequence of the start of the school day procedure.

Symbol cards or photographs of the journey to school.

Appropriate toys, for example, Lego, garage, doll's bed, etc.

Stickers or appropriate rewards.

Transition trains.

Sand timer.

Pictorial narrative.

Problems you may experience

THE CHILD DOESN'T LIKE THE PROXIMITY OF OTHERS IN THE CLOAKROOM OR CLASSROOM.

Allow the child to enter school or the classroom a few minutes before the other children, or negotiate an activity or job for the child to do in a quieter part of the school and allow him or her to enter after the class have settled.

Set up a pictorial sequence for the start of the day for this procedure.

THE CHILD DOESN'T LIKE NOISE/THE CHILD FINDS IT HARD TO SETTLE.

Allow the child to enter school or the classroom a few minutes before the other children, or negotiate an activity or job for the child to do in a quieter part of the school and allow him or her to enter after the class have settled.

Set up a pictorial sequence for the start of the day for this procedure.

Ensure a slow start to the day.

THE CHILD WILL NOT ENTER THE SCHOOL OR CLASSROOM.

Check the current entry activity for appropriateness. Modify it, if necessary – the child's interests may change quickly and without warning.

Introduce the child to the activity outside the classroom and transfer slowly to the workstation. Set up targets in small steps to reduce the time spent outside the classroom. Use a pictorial narrative, if appropriate.

Set up the pictorial sequence the night before and allow the child to take this home to share with his or her family and to be reinforced before leaving for school. Give the family a pictorial narrative.

THE CHILD DOESN'T WANT TO LEAVE THE PARENT.

Set up a pictorial start of the school day sequence with the parent, to start from leaving home and time to leave the parent. The parent should give the sequence strip to school staff on arrival. A sand timer or transition trains might be needed to reinforce.

Use a pictorial narrative at home and school.

Negotiate an appropriate entry time – before or after the class have arrived.

Allow the child to bring a toy from home. Negotiate a storage place for the day; for example, put a car in a garage or a doll/teddy in a bed. Agree a place where the toy is in sight but not accessible until home time.

Distract with the 'Happy Scrap Book' (see p.29).

THE CHILD INSISTS ON BRINGING TOYS TO SCHOOL.

Allow child to bring a toy from home. Negotiate a storage place for the day; for example, put a car in a garage or a doll/teddy in a bed. Agree a place where the toy is in sight but not accessible until home time.

THE CHILD BECOMES UPSET BY A CHANGE OF ROUTE TO SCHOOL.

Introduce a pictorial sequence of the route, or give the child a map with the usual route indicated. (Photocopy maps or use colour coding to change the route.)

Use a pictorial narrative to explain possible changes.

Change one picture at a time or modify the map to vary the route in small steps.

Go through the revised route with the child before leaving home.

Additional verbal warnings may be necessary before the sequence is changed.

3. School assemblies

How to prepare the child

Stage 1 Visit the assembly hall while it is empty.

Stage 2 Read the pictorial narrative. Show the symbol strip to show the routine. Walk to the assembly hall. Allow the child to sit at the side of the class, where he or she can be taken out easily, if necessary. Limit the child's time in the hall and increase it slowly by using a sand timer.

What you might need

Symbol cards for:

quiet

walk

sing

listen

good sitting

good looking

good listening

good singing

classroom.

Strip to attach symbols.

Problems you may experience

THE CHILD DOESN'T LIKE NOISE.

Limit the child's participation in the assembly using a sand timer. Gradually increase the time to de-sensitise the child.

Use transition trains to prepare the child for going to the assembly hall. Allow the child to leave before the singing or clapping. Reward good behaviour immediately using motivational chart stickers.

THE CHILD DOESN'T LIKE THE CLOSE PROXIMITY OF CHILDREN AND CROWDS.

Decide on a place – the back or side of the class or assembly hall. Introduce the child to a cushion and place this at his or her place. Allow the child to enter the hall before the other children. If appropriate, gradually move the cushion closer to the class group.

THE CHILD CANNOT SIT THROUGHOUT ASSEMBLY.

Limit the assembly time. Increase the participation time by adding symbols of the assembly routine one at a time. A sand timer could be used to support this. Reinforce success with a sticker or reward.

THE CHILD WILL NOT ATTEND ASSEMBLY WHEN VISITORS ARE PRESENT.

Prepare the child in advance. Read a story or discuss photographs relating to the visitor and his or her role. Introduce the visitor through a symbol or photograph on the assembly routine strip.

THE CHILD COMMENTS ALOUD OR OUT OF TURN.

Read the pictorial narrative for appropriate behaviour during assembly time. Show the 'quiet' symbol before entering the hall. Take the symbol to the hall to reinforce this. Use stickers or a reward for successful assembly times.

THE CHILD DOESN'T LIKE LARGE SPACES.

Allow the child to have his or her own cushion or small space in the hall.

THE CHILD HAS DIFFICULTY WALKING IN LINE TO THE ASSEMBLY HALL.

Introduce a photographic sequence of lining up (the child standing at the front or rear of line). Go through this with the child before he or she leaves the classroom. Use stickers or a reward for good walking in line.

THE CHILD FINDS CHANGES IN ROUTINE DIFFICULT.

Use a symbol strip to show the sequence of assembly routine. Take it to the hall with you. Remove the symbols as each part finishes. Use transition trains or a sand timer to prepare the child for the return to the classroom.

4. Playtimes

How to prepare the child

Stage 1 Introduce the symbol cards and other equipment – for example, transition trains or a sand timer – for outside play and show the sequence.

Stage 2 Visit the playground, when unused, to observe the area, playground games or markings, etc. Match it with symbol cards and selected equipment. Ensure that you give the child prior warning of the end of playtime.

Stage 3 Explain the playground rules. Read a pictorial narrative for these or a general one on playtimes, if appropriate. You may need to introduce a turn taking system or a choosing board at this stage and practise the routine with a group first.

Stage 4 Repeat the above routine for a normal playtime, with others.

A pictorial narrative and relevant symbol cards will be needed to be prepared for indoor playtimes on bad weather days.

What you might need

Symbol cards for:

> play
>
> playground
>
> lining up
>
> classroom/hall/dining room
>
> outside play
>
> inside play
>
> coat, gloves, scarf, etc.
>
> game
>
> playground equipment
>
> help
>
> whistle/bell.

Visual representation of playground rules.

Visual representation of sharing or turn taking.

Choosing board.

Strip to attach symbols to show the routine or rules.

Transition trains.

Sand timer.

Problems you may experience

THE CHILD DOESN'T LIKE THE PROXIMITY OF OTHERS IN THE PLAYGROUND.

Allow the child to go to the playground a few minutes before the other children.

If possible, give the child his or her own space in the playground.

Slowly introduce other children to the area for organised games.

THE CHILD DOESN'T LIKE THE NOISE.

Limit the child's participation in the playground. Withdraw him or her to a quieter area until playtime has finished. Use ear protectors.

THE CHILD DISRUPTS PEER GAMES. THE CHILD IS AGGRESSIVE TOWARDS OTHERS IN THE PLAYGROUND.

Read a pictorial narrative or role play with puppets to demonstrate appropriate playground behaviour and reinforce playground rules.

Consider visual turn taking materials and a 'buddy system' to model appropriate behaviour. The 'buddy system', in this instance, is where a child with an ASD is paired with one or more other children in order to help with understanding and co-operation, and to foster social skills. This usually takes place during playtimes (especially outdoor play), on school trips and when working on special projects.

Use a 'can I play?' card and demonstrate how the child should approach his or her peers to play.

Reward good/gentle playing.

WET PLAYTIMES.

Introduce a pictorial narrative.

Read this before the indoor playtime.

Introduce the revised symbol strip to the child or change the symbols together.

Use a choosing board or turn taking support materials. Continue the buddy system, if in place.

THE CHILD DOESN'T WANT TO COME INTO SCHOOL AT THE END OF PLAYTIME.

Add a motivator symbol to the end of the routine strip. Refer to the strip to remind the child of the expected behaviour.

Use a reward system for coming in.

Ensure that the child is given adequate warning of the end of playtime – use a sand timer or the transition trains system, to reinforce the verbal warning.

THE CHILD DOESN'T WANT TO GO OUT TO PLAY.

Limit the child's involvement in playtimes and gradually increase the time outside. Use a sand timer to show the agreed time. Reinforce with a motivator or reward.

Introduce the buddy system.

UNEXPECTED END TO PLAYTIME; FOR EXAMPLE, BAD WEATHER OR FIRE DRILL.

Have an emergency symbol or routine strip accessible, such as 'lining up' or 'lining up, classroom'.

Practise times of stopping to the whistle/bell and then continuing with playtime. Show the 'play' symbol when playtime is resumed.

Introduce a pictorial narrative to explain possible changes to playtime routines.

5. Play/activity/choosing times

How to prepare the child

Stage 1 Introduce the choosing symbol on the visual timetable. Explain the length of time of the activity and turn taking system, if used. Read a pictorial narrative if appropriate.

Stage 2 At choosing time, show the choosing board or box and invite the child to choose from it. If the board is used, remove the photograph or symbol from it as the child makes his or her choice.

Stage 3. Display the sand timer to show the agreed length of the choosing time.

Stage 4 Encourage the child to focus on his or her choice. If agreed, the child can re-select from the remaining photographs or symbols. Give the child a verbal warning, while referring to the visual indicator, prior to the end of choosing time.

Alternative routine. The child can make his or her choices from the board or box at the beginning of the day and attach the photograph or symbol next to the choosing symbol on the visual timetable.

What you might need

Symbol cards for choose/choosing to attach to the visual timetable.

Visual representation of sharing or turn taking, such as a strip of children's photographs/names in the sequence of their turn.

Choosing board with a selection of choosing resources in photographic or symbol form; *or* choosing box with a selection of resources.

Transition trains.

Sand timer.

Pictorial narrative.

Problems you may experience

THE CHILD DOESN'T LIKE SHARING RESOURCES.

Practice turn taking games, initially with an adult and then with one child, and extend to group situations.

Introduce a visual strip with children's photographs/names in the sequence of their turn. Remove the photograph after the child has had his or her turn and place it at the end of the sequence, or attach a photograph or symbol of the child using the resource to the box.

Use a sand timer and the transition trains system to indicate length of choosing time and the time to change over.

Use a pictorial narrative if needed.

THE CHILD DOES NOT LIKE THE PROXIMITY OF OTHERS.

Allow the child to have his or her own space for choosing. Help the child to become used to the proximity of others by carrying out the following steps.

Sit next to child, initially to observe.

Run a commentary on the child's play.

Use parallel play.

Invite another child to use parallel play.

When appropriate, share out the equipment between two or more children and begin with parallel play, moving on to developing shared or co-operative play.

THE CHILD'S FOCUS ON HIS OR HER CHOICE IS LIMITED.

Limit the choice of resources or allow the child to select one resource for the entire choosing time.

Use a sand timer to show the agreed choosing time with the one resource, before changing.

Involve other children to model play skills.

THE CHILD DOESN'T WANT CHOOSING TIME TO FINISH.

Refer to the visual timetable before choosing time, to show the following activity.

Use a reward for 'good finishing' or 'good tidying up'.

Ensure that the child is given adequate warning of the end of choosing time – more than one, if possible. Use a sand timer or the transition trains system to reinforce the verbal warning.

Use additional winding down routines, such as counting down with the digits displayed and then a symbol to indicate the next activity.

Use a pictorial narrative if necessary.

THE CHILD FINDS IT DIFFICULT TO CHOOSE.

Limit the choices on the choosing board or in the box. Offer a choice of two until the child is able to make his or her selection confidently.

Ensure that one of the choices is a favourite.

Give a sticker or reward for 'good choosing'.

Allow the child to make his or her selection at the beginning of the day and attach the choice to the timetable.

THE CHILD ALWAYS CHOOSES THE SAME RESOURCES.

Use a visual strip to indicate 'It's [name of child]'s turn to choose', so that a variety of resources are used. Rotate turns. The adult should model this initially and then involve the child's peers.

Change one photograph/symbol each time on the choosing board or one resource in the box.

Negotiate a change of resource, with the favourites kept for a special choosing session at the end of the day.

6. P.E. lessons/gym class

How to prepare the child

Stage 1 Read the pictorial narrative.

Stage 2 Visit the hall or P.E. area, look at the equipment and match it to the symbol.

Stage 3 Arrange a short individual session in an empty hall. Introduce the symbol strip, with 'stop' and 'finish' incorporated. Practise the undressing routine. If appropriate, use a separate dressing sequence strip. Walk to the hall. Take the symbol strip with you. Use additional markers, such as transition trains or a sand timer, to prepare for the end of the session. Practise dressing and returning to the classroom.

Stage 4 Allow the child to participate in the class session. Limit participation time, if appropriate.

Stage 5 Continue to increase the length of participation until the child is fully involved in all lessons.

What you might need

Symbol cards for:

dressing

undressing

walk, stand, sit

quiet

stop

finish

sharing

game, climbing, running, jumping, etc.

good listening, good looking

large and small equipment

hall, playground, outside.

Visual sequence strip to show the order of dressing.

Transition trains.

Sand timer.

Pictorial narrative – this can also be used to outline the rules of a game or activity.

Problems you may experience

THE CHILD DOESN'T LIKE LARGE SPACES.

Allow the child to enter the hall a few minutes before the other children.

Give the child his or her own space with a physical boundary – use chairs or a hoop/hoops, or mark the floor/ground to indicate his or her space.

THE CHILD FINDS SHARING DIFFICULT.

Practise turn taking with small and large equipment in the classroom and the playground. Adult to partner, initially, to model appropriate turn taking.

Introduce additional visual resources to show turn taking, using photos or names of peers. Refer to the appropriate photo and say, 'It's [name of child]'s turn.'

Introduce a pictorial narrative.

THE CHILD IS NOISY AND EXCITABLE.

Read a pictorial narrative outlining acceptable behaviour before going into the hall. (This can be done with all the class.) Reinforce the agreed consequences for noisy behaviour in the hall, for example a 1, 2 or 3 minute time out.

Use a 'quiet' symbol as a reminder throughout the lesson.

Follow the agreed strategies until the child is quiet.

Use a reward chart for quiet behaviour.

THE CHILD DOESN'T WANT TO GET DRESSED.

Add a motivator symbol to the end of the routine strip. Refer to the strip to remind the child of the expected behaviour.

Use a reward system, such as a star or tick for each completed dressing task on the sequence strip.

Use additional reinforcers, such as the sand timer or transition trains.

THE CHILD DOESN'T WANT TO GET UNDRESSED.

Break down the undressing stage, repeating Stage 3 until the child is ready to move on to Stage 4.

Use a reward system for each stage.

THE CHILD FINDS IT DIFFICULT TO LISTEN TO INSTRUCTIONS/FOLLOW THE SAFETY RULES.

Ensure that the rules are displayed in the P.E./gym area.

Read a pictorial narrative highlighting the rules before going into the hall. Reinforce the agreed consequences for non-compliance.

Use additional symbol cards to reinforce the rules at the beginning of and throughout the lesson, including 'good looking' and 'good listening'.

Use a sand timer or the transition trains system.

Use a reward system for rule compliance.

FIRE DRILL OR EMERGENCY EVACUATION OF THE HALL DURING A LESSON.

Have an emergency routine strip accessible in the P.E. area, such as 'stop', 'walk' and 'playground'. Refer to the 'stop' symbol.

Practise games where the children stop actions quickly.

Introduce a pictorial narrative or fire alarm song (see p.111).

Practise evacuation procedures frequently.

7. Swimming lessons

How to prepare the child

Stage 1 Introduce the symbol cards and prepare the child for a visit to the swimming pool. (A pictorial narrative may need to be read at this stage.)

Stage 2 Visit the pool when unused to observe the dressing area, the shower, the pool and any other relevant equipment. Match these with symbol cards.

Stage 3 Visit the pool to observe it in use. Sit at the side.

Stage 4 Practise the dressing routine in school, using the symbol strip.

Stage 5 Visit the pool, get changed and sit at the side.

Stage 6 Visit the pool, get changed and use the shower.

Stage 7 Attach all the symbols to the routine strip. Remind the child of the pool rules. Visit the pool, use the shower and enter the water.

Give the child a warning before he or she has to get out of the water, for example the transition train.

What you might need

Symbol cards for:

> swimming pool
>
> walk
>
> shower
>
> time to get out
>
> dressing.

Strip to attach the symbols to show the routine.

Visual sequence strip to show the order of dressing.

Transition trains.

Sand timer.

Pictorial narrative.

Problems you may experience

THE CHILD DOESN'T LIKE THE PROXIMITY OF OTHERS IN THE POOL OR DRESSING ROOM.

Allow the child to enter the dressing room or pool a few minutes before the other children.

Give the child his or her own space in the dressing room and the pool.

THE CHILD DOESN'T LIKE NOISE.

Limit the child's participation in the lesson using a sand timer.

Withdraw him or her to a quieter area until the lesson has finished.

Gradually increase the time spent at the pool.

THE CHILD IS NOISY AND EXCITABLE IN THE POOL.

Ensure that the pool rules are displayed in the dressing area and in the pool. Refer to the rules before the lesson.

Use a symbol card to remind the child to be quiet.

THE CHILD DOESN'T LIKE THE SHOWER.

Allow the child to stand in the shower when it is turned off.

Allow the child to feel the water on his or her hands or feet and then move on to other body parts. A sequence strip of body parts could be introduced so that this action can be broken down into small steps.

Give a reverse countdown for the time spent in the shower.

THE CHILD DOESN'T WANT TO GET DRESSED.

Add a motivator symbol to the end of the routine strip. Refer to the strip to remind the child of the expected behaviour.

Use a reward system, such as a star or tick, for each completed dressing task on the sequence strip.

Use additional reinforcers, such as the sand timer or transition trains.

Introduce a pictorial narrative if necessary.

THE CHILD DOESN'T WANT TO GET UNDRESSED.

Break down the undressing stage, repeating Stage 4 until the child is ready to move on to Stage 5. Use a reward system for each stage.

THE CHILD DOESN'T WANT TO GET OUT OF THE POOL.

Refer to the pool rules.

Use a sand timer or the transition trains system.

Use a reward system for rule compliance.

Introduce a pictorial narrative.

THERE IS A FIRE DRILL OR EMERGENCY EVACUATION OF THE POOL DURING A LESSON.

Have an emergency routine strip accessible in the pool area, such as 'time to get out' and 'playground'. Refer to the 'time to get out' symbol.

Practise games where the children get out of the water quickly.

Introduce a pictorial narrative.

Practise evacuation procedures frequently.

8. Obsessions

How to prepare the child

Stage 1 Introduce a pictorial obsession to explain the term obsession and agreed routine for using these in school.

Stage 2 Discuss times when obsessions will be included on the school timetable and storage of any resources in connection with these at other times. (Obsessions make good motivators and rewards.)

Stage 3 Add a symbol to the visual timetable to indicate times when obsessions will be allowed.

Stage 4 Introduce 'obsession' time. Use a sand timer to indicate the length of time agreed.

Stage 5 Give a verbal or visual warning a few minutes before the end of obsession time.

Stage 6 Replace any resources in the agreed storage area until home time or the next obsession time.

What you might need

Symbol of obsession, for example, drawing flags, looking at timetables, etc.

Sand timer.

Transition trains.

Visual timetable.

Pictorial narrative.

It is not a good idea to attempt to eliminate obsessions, unless they are inappropriate. Unacceptable ones may replace acceptable obsessions. Obsessions can be used as motivators and rewards.

Problems you may experience

THE CHILD RESISTS THE END OF 'OBSESSION' TIME.

Ensure that the consequences of not ending 'obsession' time are included in the pictorial narrative. Refer to this at the end of the agreed time.

Use transition trains or a counting down system to reinforce that the end of 'obsession' time is approaching.

Ensure that any resources are stored where the child can see them but that he or she does not have access to them outside the agreed times. A high shelf is suitable.

THE RESOURCES ARE STORED WITHIN THE CHILD'S SIGHT, BUT THEY BECOME A DISTRACTION OR THE CHILD ATTEMPTS TO ACCESS THEM OUTSIDE THE AGREED 'OBSESSION' TIMES.

Use a box with the child's name or photograph. At the end of 'obsession' time show the child a photograph or symbol of the storage place out of sight before putting the box away.

If appropriate, allow the child to accompany the adult to put the box away.

Introduce a brief group activity at the end of 'obsession' time, in which all the children replace the resources in boxes to be put away in the storage places. Visual symbols or photographs could be used to indicate the storage places.

THE CHILD BRINGS RESOURCES FROM HOME FOR 'OBSESSION' TIME.

Allow the child a brief time at the beginning of the morning with the resources.

Ensure that this is indicated on the visual timetable.

Use a sand timer and possibly additional visual resources to indicate the length of time agreed.

Agree a storage space for the resources until the next 'obsession' time or home time.

If necessary, use a pictorial narrative to reinforce the arrangement.

THE OBSESSION CHANGES.

Replace the existing timetable symbol with one for the new obsession.

If the new obsession is less acceptable, consider ways of introducing a modified version; for example, if the obsession is opening doors, encourage looking at or collecting pictures of doors, making models of doors to open, etc.

If the new obsession is unacceptable, a pictorial narrative could be introduced to explain the unacceptability of the obsession and ideas for school 'obsession' time.

THERE IS A PLANNED TIMETABLE CHANGE DURING THE USUAL 'OBSESSION' TIME.

Ensure that there is an alternative time for 'obsession' time.

Explain the changes to the child. It may be a good idea to have a narrative prepared for these times.

Change the visual timetable.

Use a question mark on the timetable if you are unsure whether there will be a change of time.

Ensure that all cover staff know about the agreed 'obsession' time and the importance of including it in the child's timetable.

THERE IS AN UNPLANNED TIMETABLE CHANGE DURING THE USUAL 'OBSESSION' TIME.

Use a narrative to explain the changes to the timetable.

Refer to the visual timetable and alter it to include an 'obsession' time as soon as possible after the change.

It may be necessary to adapt the length of 'obsession' time to allow for unsettled behaviour.

Ensure that all cover staff know about the agreed 'obsession' time and the importance of including it in the child's timetable.

9. Staffing changes

How to prepare the child

Stage 1 Introduce a pictorial narrative to explain that staff members change at times.

Stage 2 Discuss the change of staff member/s at school.

Stage 3 Create a 'My New Teacher' book with the child. If possible, include a photograph of the new staff member.

Stage 4 Continue to add pages, or make an additional book, to include any known changes to the routine or classroom layout. Attach photographs wherever possible.

Negotiate consistency of routine and workstation location, etc. with the new member of staff and reassure the child that this will remain consistent. Invite the child to share the book with his or her family.

Stage 5 If possible, allow the child to meet the new member of staff and share his or her visual resources, workstation, etc. with that member of staff before the change.

What you might need

Photographs of new staff members.

Photographs of any modifications to timetables or classroom layout.

Pictorial narrative.

Problems you may experience

THE CHILD ARRIVES AT SCHOOL TO FIND THAT HIS OR HER USUAL TEACHER IS ABSENT AND A SUPPLY TEACHER OR TA IS LEADING THE CLASS.

Keep a narrative available to explain the teacher's absence. Include a page to show the teacher for the day *or* have a permanent laminated card at the child's workstation which reads: 'My teacher today is …………………………' with the teacher's name and/or photo attached.

If possible, have a bank of ready-made name cards or photographs of supply teachers, for quick use.

Reassure the child that his or her routine will remain consistent.

THE CHILD ENTERS THE CLASSROOM, BUT BECOMES AGITATED BY THE CHANGES.

Modify the approach, length of sessions, type of activity and work expectations. This can be done with sand timers or transition trains without altering the visual timetable.

Reinforce successful steps with stickers or an agreed reward.

Refer to the 'Happy Scrap Book' (p.29) to distract and redirect the mood.

THE TEACHER HAS A PLANNED ABSENCE FROM SCHOOL.

Read a narrative relating to the teacher's absence in advance.

Change the teacher's name/photograph in the book or on the laminated card, with the child, before he or she leaves school on the day before the absence. (An alternative card can be made to read: 'My teacher tomorrow will be …………………………' and then replaced on the following morning with the card reading: 'My teacher today is …………………………')

Or introduce a 'days of the week' visual symbol strip and attach the name or photograph of the supply teacher to the relevant day/s.

Modify for an INA's planned absence.

THE CHILD RESISTS ENTRY TO SCHOOL ON THE DAY OF THE STAFF ABSENCE.

Read the narrative and show the laminated card to the child outside the classroom.

Go through the visual timetable to show the child that his or her routine is consistent.

If necessary, use transition trains to modify the length of class participation and introduce longer workstation sessions.

Reinforce with stickers or agreed rewards.

Refer to the 'Happy Scrap Book' if anxiety levels remain high. Retire to a safe haven with the child.

UNEXPECTED STAFF CHANGES DURING THE SCHOOL DAY.

Follow the suggestions for an unplanned staff absence as soon as possible following the change.

Modify the approach if the child shows agitation.

Explain the circumstances to parents or inform home through the home/school diary or e-mail.

10. End of term/school year

How to prepare the child

Stage 1 At least one week before the end of term, read a pictorial narrative to prepare the child for end of term changes and the forthcoming school holiday.

Stage 2 At the end of a week or the beginning of the last week of term, introduce a 'days of the week' symbol strip and attach any additional activities or changes to activities to the relevant day.

Stage 3 Refer to the strip at the beginning of each day. Remove the activity symbols for the day and add them to the appropriate place on the visual timetable.

At the end of the day, remove the day of the week symbol from the strip and talk about the following day.

Parents could use a similar strip to show activities planned for the school holiday.

What you might need

Symbol cards for end of term and holiday activities.

Strip to attach symbols, to show the routine.

Transition trains.

Sand timer.

Pictorial narrative.

Problems you may experience

PLANNED ACTIVITIES CHANGE AT SHORT NOTICE.

On the visual timetable introduce the idea of an unknown event by using a question mark symbol. Read a pictorial narrative explaining unexpected changes in routine/activity (see Chapter 13).

As soon as possible set up a revised timetable with the child and discuss the changes.

Repeat the pictorial narrative.

THE CHILD RESISTS PARTICIPATION IN THE END OF TERM ACTIVITIES.

Prepare the child in advance for the activity.

Use pictures, symbols, artefacts, visits to other parts of the school, etc., to reinforce activity expectations.

If appropriate, practise games, etc. in a one-to-one with an adult or with a small group of children.

Use role modelling.

Refer to the activity on the timetable to show the child the time and place.

If resistance persists, allow the child to be an observer or to take a minor or modified part in the activity.

THE CHILD BECOMES OVER-EXCITED BY THE END OF TERM ACTIVITIES.

Read a pictorial narrative to show the rules and expectations associated with the activities.

Use mobile individual symbol cards to reinforce the rules during the activities.

Introduce a calming activity, in a quiet area, for example the library or workstation, to give the child time to settle before rejoining the class.

THE CHILD BECOMES MORE ANXIOUS AS THE END OF TERM APPROACHES.

Provide parents with a pictorial narrative and/or revised timetable or 'days of the week' strip to reinforce changes. Negotiate a holiday activity strip with the parents and go through this, when appropriate, during the school day.

Use additional visuals, such as a calendar, to show the child the date for returning to school.

Allow the child to set up his or her workstation on the last day of term, for the day of return. Reassure the child that his or her workstation and routine will remain consistent in the new term.

CHANGES TO STAFFING OR CHILDREN IN THE NEW TERM.

If possible, prepare the child for any changes before the end of the previous term.

Make a book or pictorial narrative, which introduces the changes.

Reinforce that the child's workstation and personal routine will remain consistent.

Invite parents to be involved. Make additional copies of books and visual resources, and suggest that these are referred to and discussed, at home, during the holiday.

Set up the workstation, with the child, on the last day of term, for the day of return.

THE CHILD DOESN'T WANT TO TAKE NARRATIVES OR VISUAL STRIPS HOME.

Invite the child to take photographs of his or her workstation set up for the new term.

Suggest that he or she shares these with family members.

Make a different book for home use.

The Fire Bell

Use this song to prepare children for the sound of the fire alarm – very short bursts to begin with, at the end of the song.

The fire bell is a good thing,
If smoke is around it starts to ring.
It rings quite loud,
It rings quite long,
I wish it would just sing a song.

The fire bell is a good thing,
If fire's around it starts to ring.
It makes us jump,
It makes us start,
I hear the beating of my heart.

The fire bell is a good thing,
It keeps us safe when it starts to ring.
I'll try to smile
I will stay calm,
Then I'll be safe from any harm.

The fire bell is a good thing,
I'll remember that if it starts to ring.
It rings quite loud
To keep me well,
So thank you Mr Fire Bell!

(Goes well with 'can-can' music – 'The Galop' from Offenbach's *Orpheus in the Underworld*)

The Final Word

There are still many teachers and parents who remain unconvinced about inclusion of children with ASD in the mainstream classroom. Without knowledge, understanding, preparation and planning even the most experienced and accommodating of teachers can end up feeling de-skilled.

We hope this book will help to empower schools and teachers. We also hope that it will make a real difference to those children with ASDs, and their caregivers, as they attempt to find their proper place and entitlement in the educational system.

We have witnessed at first hand how the strategies outlined in this book can benefit most children and so making inclusion a success for the child with an ASD will have the added bonus of helping all children in the mainstream classroom.